Editors

Rebecca Wood

Erica N. Russikoff, M.A.

Illustrator

Mark Mason

Cover Artists

Kevin Barnes

Barb Lorseyedi

Editor in Chief

Ina Massler Levin, M.A.

Creative Director

Karen J. Goldfluss, M.S. Ed.

Art Coordinator

Renée Christine Yates

Imaging

Rosa C. See

Publisher

Mary D. Smith, M.S. Ed.

Author

Garth Sundem, M.M.

The classroom teacher may reproduce copies of materials in this book for classroom use only. Reproduction of any part for an entire school or school system is strictly prohibited. No part of this publication may be transmitted, stored, or recorded in any form without written permission from the publisher.

Teacher Created Resources, Inc.

6421 Industry Way

Westminster, CA 92683

www.teachercreated.com

ISBN: 978-1-4206-2561-5

© 2009 Teacher Created Resources, Inc.

Made in U.S.A.

Table of Contents

Table of Contents *(cont.)*

Introduction

Welcome to *Puzzles and Games That Make Kids Think.* This book contains over 180 puzzles and games of more than 30 different types, each of which is not only fun, but also asks students to use their minds to figure out the solution. (There are no "word finds" here!) Students will find some of these puzzles difficult, while other puzzles will be easy. Some puzzles will take seconds, while others might take half an hour. All of the puzzles are a workout for the brain! Here are a few reasons why we think you'll enjoy this book:

- Puzzle-based brain workouts create results. Research shows that a regimen of brainteasers can lead to higher scores on problem-solving tests.[1] Research also shows that using puzzles in the classroom can lead to increased student interest and involvement.[2]

- There are four categories of brainteasers in this book: picture, word, number, and logic, with puzzles (for individual students) and games (for pairs) for each category. Within each section, students will use diverse thinking skills—in a picture puzzle, students may draw lines on a geometric figure, and in a number puzzle, they may need to read complex directions. The wide variety of puzzles keeps students engaged and entertained.

- Each page of this book includes all of the needed directions and materials (other than writing utensils!), making it easy to distribute these puzzles to early finishers. Or, you may choose to copy and distribute puzzles as part of a reward system or weekly brain-buster challenge. Students will look forward to these fun puzzles, and you can rest assured that your classroom time will be spent productively. Another use of these puzzles is to spice up homework packets—strategically insert a puzzle or two to keep things lively!

- With a less experienced class, you may need to preview puzzle directions ahead of time (especially the two-person games and logic puzzles). Consider exploring the directions as a class before independent work time. Or, explain that reading and understanding the instructions is the first part of the puzzle! Because puzzle types repeat, students will gain more confidence in their ability to solve the puzzles as they spend more time with this book.

Be careful—these puzzles are addictive, and you can easily find yourself whiling away a prep period with pencil in hand!

[1] Howard, P. J. (1994). *The Owner's Manual for the Brain.* Charlotte, NC: Leornian Press.

[2] Finke, R. A., et al. (1992). *Creative Cognition: Theory, Research, and Applications.* Cambridge, MA: The MIT Press.

Puzzle Hints

Game Hints

Some games require the ability to read and understand somewhat tricky directions. Consider previewing directions with students beforehand. Also notice that some games require photocopying the page (or allowing students to cut shapes or game boards from the book). With less experienced classes, you might play a full-class version of a game (teacher versus students) before allowing pairs to work independently. In hopes of keeping game directions brief and student friendly, many of the more intuitive directions have been omitted. If students have questions about game mechanics, encourage them to use their common sense.

Picture Puzzles

- *Map Madness!:* Make sure you start at the correct point. Then, follow the route with your finger.

- *Picture Perfect:* Imagine a grid overlaying the picture, and search only one area at a time.

- *Shape Find:* First, imagine the shape in your mind. Then, try to work around the figure systematically. And don't forget the whole figure itself!

- *Shapes All Around:* Squint! By removing distractions, the shapes will pop out.

- *Split Shapes:* Usually the lines are drawn from corners. Start there first.

- *Spun Shapes:* Imagine the first shape spun around the face of a clock. As it spins, which of the other shapes does it match? There is one shape that is different.

- *That's Not an Animal!:* Look for body parts borrowed from another animal (for example, a hippo with antlers).

- *What's Different?:* Pretend there is a grid over each picture, and confine your search to only one box at a time.

Word Puzzles

- *Colorful Foods/Animals:* This is hard! Look at all of the foods/animals in order, and circle the ones that start with the correct letter.

- *Crack the Code:* Fill in each box in order. If you're running out of time, you can usually guess the answer before finishing the last couple of boxes.

- *Crossword:* Use the given letter to help you. Do the easy ones first. Then, use those letters to help you determine the more difficult ones.

- *Crossword Challenge:* The only way to do this is to guess and check. Start by adding the first word wherever you can, and then try to make the rest fit. Write lightly in pencil in case you have to erase the words and start again!

- *Fronts and Backs:* Start with one "front" and then try it with each "back." Repeat this with each "front" on the list. Check off the "fronts" as you finish them.

- *Help Mr. Mallard:* Start at the left side of the picture and work toward the right. Each time you see a new "thing," ask yourself what letter it starts with. This way, when you get to the picture's right edge, you will know that you have found everything!

Puzzle Hints (cont.)

Word Puzzles (cont.)

- *Hide and Seek:* Scan the sentence slowly, looking for the names of different animals.

- *Letter Scramble:* Play with the vowel—it's usually the key.

- *Missing Letter:* Try the missing letter in every position, starting at the front and working your way through the word.

- *Transformers:* Look at the last word. What letter from this word could be inserted in the first word to make a new word? Repeat until you get to the bottom.

- *Word Circles:* Most words start next to the vowel. Look there first.

Number Puzzles

- *Addition Challenge:* Start by adding big numbers and then finish with little numbers. This means you will work from the center to the outer boxes. In other words, add the nine, the eight, the seven, etc. until you get close to the number you need.

- *Fill in the Blanks:* Start on the right, with the singles digit, and then work left.

- *In Addition:* If there are two numbers in any row or column, you can find the third number. Do those first.

- *Math Path:* You will almost always add the greatest numbers. In longer puzzles, look for a path between the two greatest numbers that includes an addition sign for both.

- *Math Triangle:* If there are two numbers on any side, you can find the third. Start there.

- *Number Ladder:* What do you have to add (or subtract) to get from any number to the next?

- *Snake Race:* Keep in mind the numbers that add up to your target number. Then, look for one of those numbers in the puzzle. Start at that number and experiment with ways to move until you find the combination you need.

- *Sudoku:* If a row or column already contains two numbers, you can fill in the third. Fill those in before proceeding.

- *Thinking of a Number:* Work from the filled-in digit.

Logic Puzzles

- *Alek, Elena, and Tran:* If two people did not do something, the third must have. If someone did something, it means that no one else did it and that he or she did not do anything else. (This will help you draw **X**s on the chart.)

- *Alison's Notebook, Lisa's Sock, etc.:* Memorize the three things you are looking for (for example, + polka dots, – lightning bolts, – stars). Then scan the puzzle in order, looking for the picture that matches the description.

- *Logic Maze:* Follow your path with a pencil. Just like a regular maze, if you hit a dead end, backtrack until you have more options.

- *Odd Animal Out:* Think about starting letters, or look for things that three of the animals have in common. Maybe there's more than one answer!

- *What's Next?:* Look for the repeating pattern.

1 King Tut's Tomb

This is a picture of King Tut's tomb. Can you find seven things that do not belong? Circle all of them.

2 That's Not an Animal!

Put an **X** through the animal that is not real.

Brainstorm Game

3

Directions:

1. Find a partner. Then, look at the item on the right.

2. It is a cone, but what else could it be?

3. You have 30 seconds to write one thing it could be on your set of lines. Be creative!

4. Now, it is your partner's turn.

5. Keep going until one person takes more than 30 seconds. The other person is the winner!

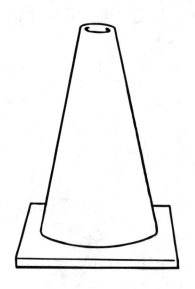

Player #1
_____
_____
_____
_____
_____
_____
_____
_____

Player #2
_____
_____
_____
_____
_____
_____
_____
_____

8 ©Teacher Created Resources, Inc.

Spun Shapes

4

Circle the shape that is not like the others.

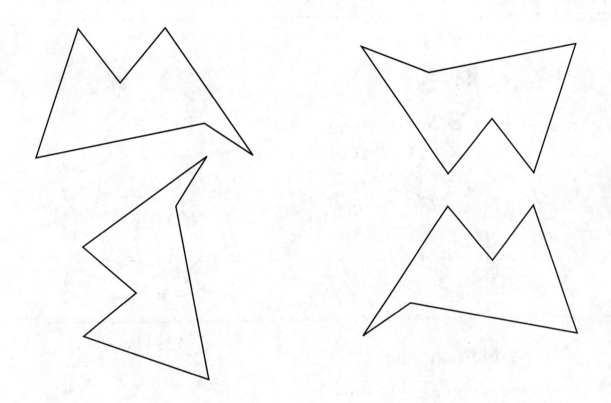

Split Shapes

5

Can you draw one line to split this shape into two triangles?

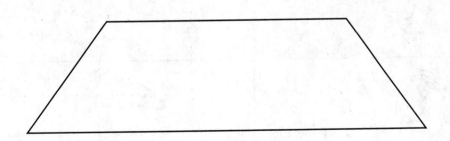

6   What's Different?

Can you spot the five differences between these two pictures? Circle the differences.

7   That's Not an Animal!

Put an **X** through the animal that is not real.

Shape Slap

8

Directions:

1. Find a partner. Look at the game board. Then, look at the shapes.

2. Pick a shape. Color in this shape on the board. If you need to, you can spin the shape. Put an **X** over the shape you used.

3. Now, it is your partner's turn.

4. The first person who does not have room to place a shape loses!

Shapes:

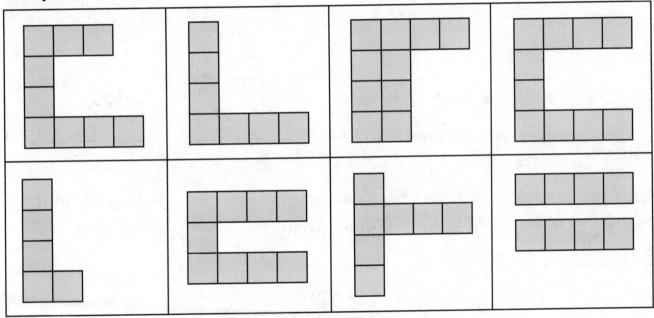

Game Board:

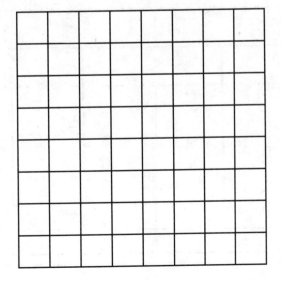

Spun Shapes

9

Circle the shape that is not like the others.

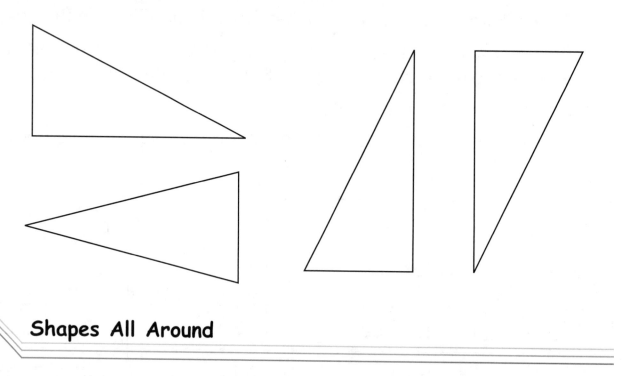

Shapes All Around

10

Can you find one triangle and nine rectangles in this picture without using the shapes more than once? Color each set of shapes a different color.

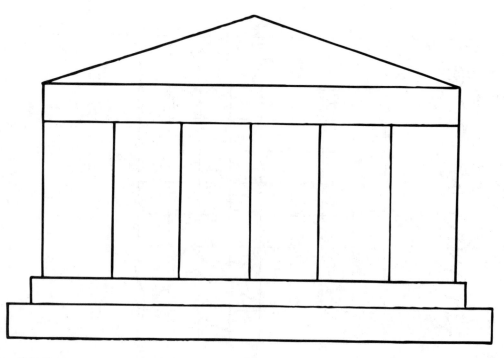

12 ©*Teacher Created Resources, Inc.*

That's Not an Animal!

11

Put an **X** through the animal that is not real.

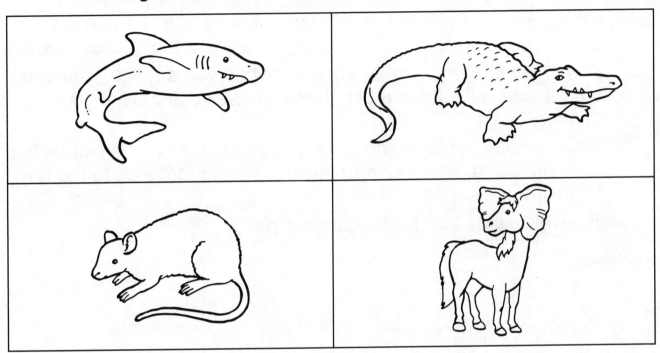

Picture Perfect

12

Circle these things: a tiger, a toucan, and an elephant.

Tangram Game

13

Directions:

1. Find a partner. Each of you will need a copy of this sheet with your own set of shapes. Cut out the shapes in the square below.

2. Look at the tangram pictures below. When you say "go," you and your partner will race to make these pictures using all of your shapes.

3. Once one of you has made a picture, cross it out. This picture is now used. Both you and your partner should move on to the next picture.

4. Whoever makes the most pictures wins!

Shapes:

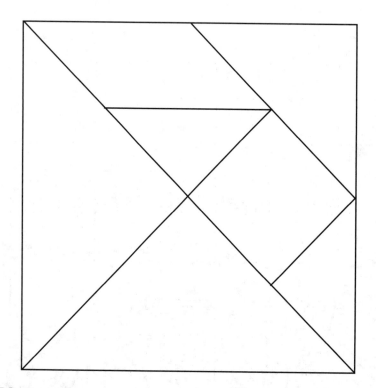

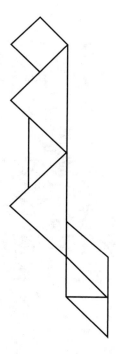

Tangram Pictures:

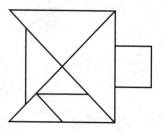
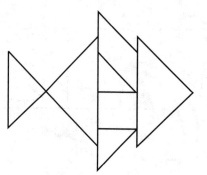

14   ©*Teacher Created Resources, Inc.*

Map Madness!

14

Do you see Pedro? He is lost! Follow the directions to get him back on track. Mark his ending spot with an **X**.

Directions:

1. ⬆ Go north on Oak St.

2. ⬅ Go west on 3rd St.

3. **END** End at the corner of Maple St.

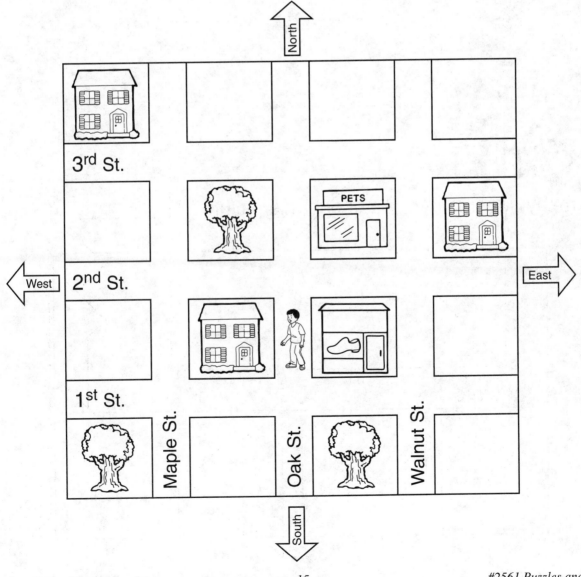

Spun Shapes

15

Circle the shape that is not like the others.

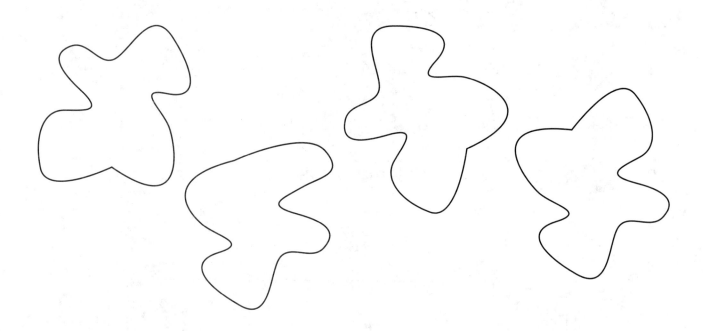

Shape Find

16

How many squares can you find in this picture? _____

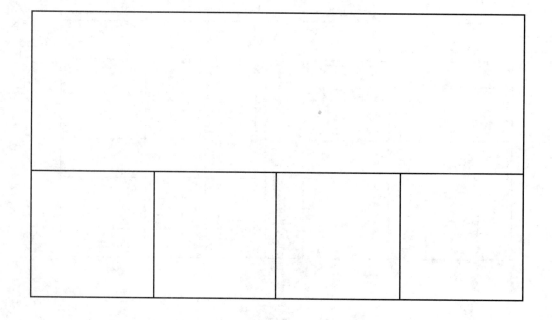

16

©Teacher Created Resources, Inc.

Split Shapes

17

Andre, Alison, and Veronica are at a birthday party. Draw lines to cut the cake so that each child gets an equal piece.

Shapes All Around

18

Can you find six rectangles in this picture? Color the rectangles.

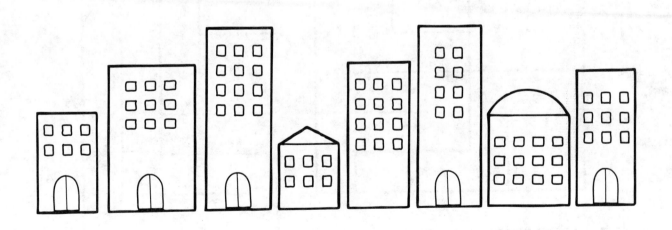

Blind Maze

19

Directions:

1. Find a partner.

2. Look at the maze below. It looks easy, but could you do it with your eyes closed?

3. Work together: the person who draws must close his or her eyes. Don't peek! The other person gives directions (right, left, forward, or back).

4. See if you can make it to "FINISH" without hitting any walls.

5. If you want, you can race other teams. Time yourselves, and add 20 seconds for every time you hit a wall.

START

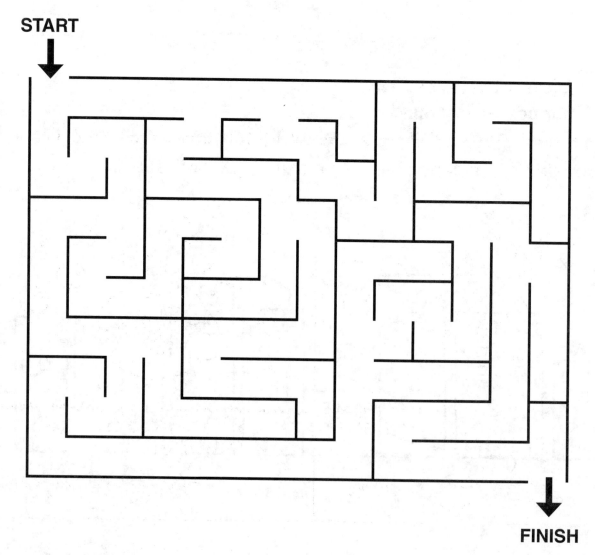

FINISH

Split Shapes

20

Can you draw one line to split this shape into four triangles?

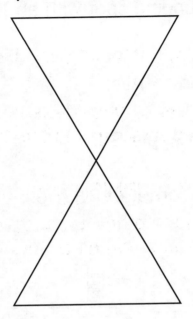

What's Different?

21

Can you spot the five differences between these two pictures? Circle the differences.

Map Madness!

Do you see Pedro? He is lost again! Follow the directions to get him back on track. Mark his ending spot with an **X**.

Directions:

1. Go north on 1ˢᵗ Ave.

2. Go east on Apple St.

3. **END** End at the corner of 3ʳᵈ Ave.

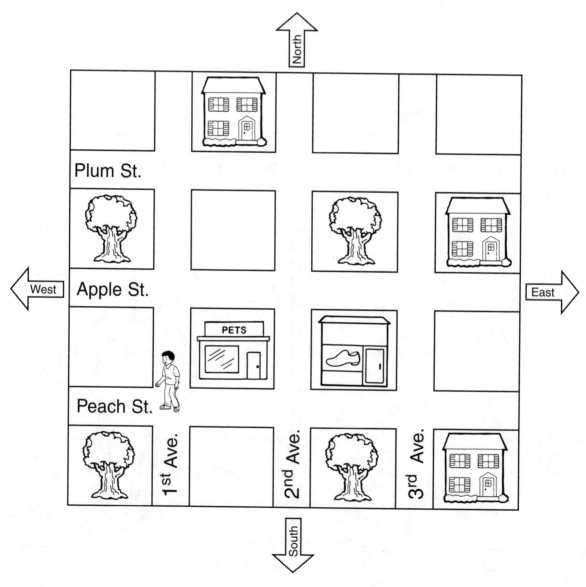

Split Shapes

23

Tina, Devon, Isabel, and Carlos are at a birthday party. Draw two lines to cut the cake so that each child gets an equal piece.

Shapes All Around

24

Can you find four triangles in this picture without using the shape more than once? Color the triangles.

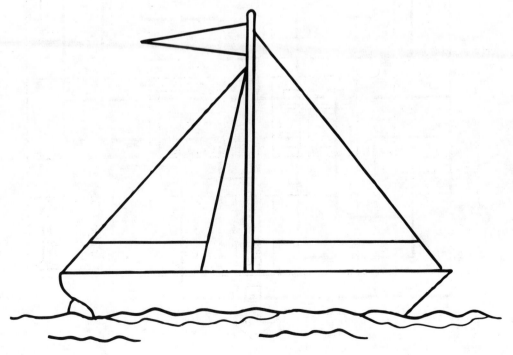

Favorite Foods Maze Game

25

Directions:

1. You will need two copies of this sheet. Find a partner and two pencils. Give a copy of this maze to your partner.

2. You will race to draw lines from each animal to its favorite food. Connect the dog to the bone and the monkey to the banana.

3. Ready, set, go!

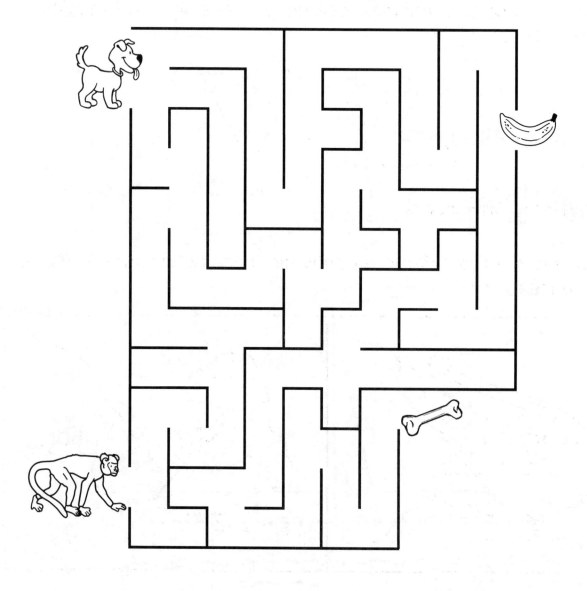

22

©*Teacher Created Resources, Inc.*

Shape Find

26

How many squares can you find in this picture? _____

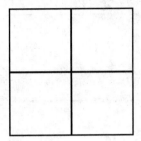

Together

27

Can you put these two triangles together to make six new triangles?
Draw the shape.

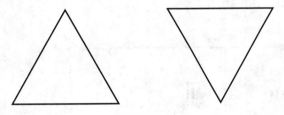

What's Different?

28

Can you spot the five differences between these two pictures? Circle
the differences.

29   **Split Shapes**

Can you draw two lines to split this shape into three triangles?

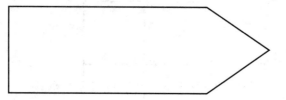

30   **Split Shapes**

Can you draw three lines to split this same shape into nine triangles?

31   **That's Not an Animal!**

Put an **X** through the animal that is not real.

Shape Find

32

How many triangles can you find in this picture? _____

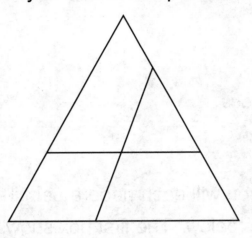

Spun Shapes

33

Circle the shape that is not like the others.

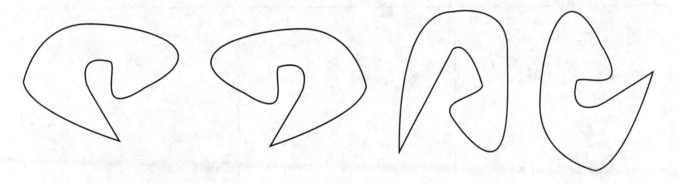

Shape Find

34

How many rectangles can you find in this picture? _____

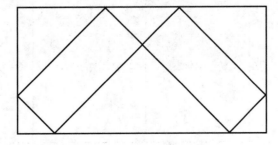

Super Stumper: Shape Find

35

How many triangles can you find in the picture from puzzle #34 _____

Cartoon Helpers

36

Directions:

1. Find a partner. You will each need a pencil.

2. Look at the boxes below. The first box shows the start of a cartoon.

3. Draw the next box. Tell your partner what happens in your box. Then, it is your partner's turn. Continue taking turns.

4. At the end, work together to tell the complete story.

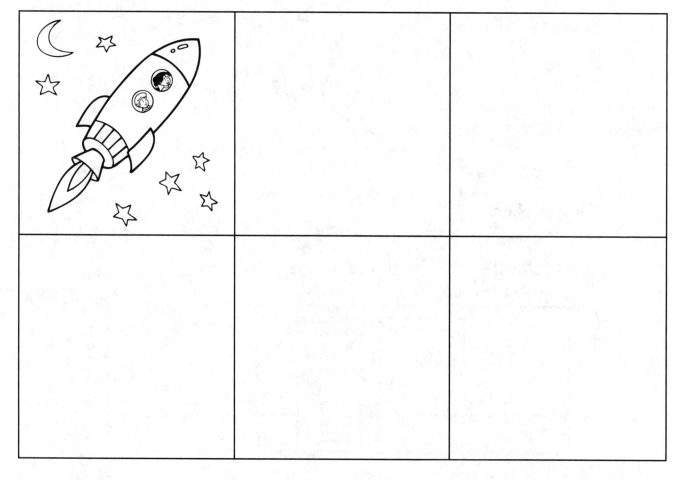

Split Shapes

37

Mike, Bruce, Brit, Carlos, Amy, and Maria are at a birthday party. Draw three lines to cut the cake so that each child gets an equal piece.

Shapes All Around

38

Can you find two triangles, four rectangles, and twelve squares in this picture without using the shapes more than once? Color each set of shapes a different color.

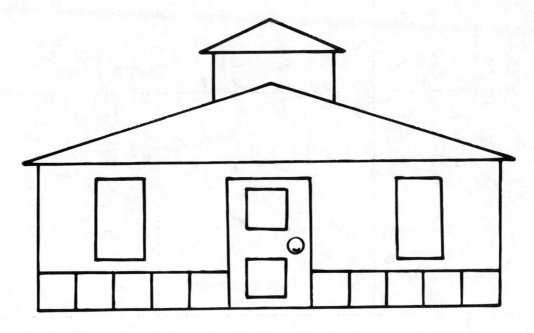

That's Not an Animal!

39

Put an **X** through the animal that is not real.

Dinosaurs

40

This is a picture taken at the time of the dinosaurs. Can you find six things that do not belong? Circle them.

Map Madness!

41

Do you see Pedro? He is lost again! Follow the directions to get him back on track. Mark his ending spot with an **X**.

Directions:

1. ⬇️ Go south on Strawberry St.

2. ➡️ Go east on Pine St.

3. **END** End at the corner of Cherry St.

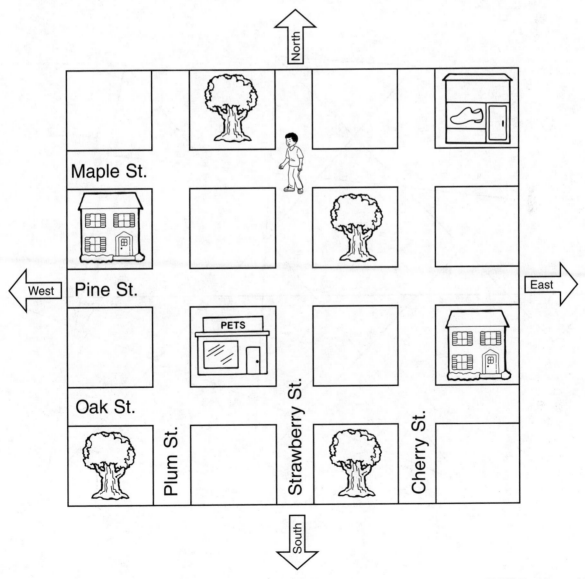

Triangle Take-Away Game

42

Directions:

1. Find a partner.

2. Put a blank piece of paper over the picture below, and trace it lightly in pencil.

3. Take turns erasing a line. You can erase a long or short line. But, you must leave at least one triangle.

4. The first person who cannot leave a triangle loses.

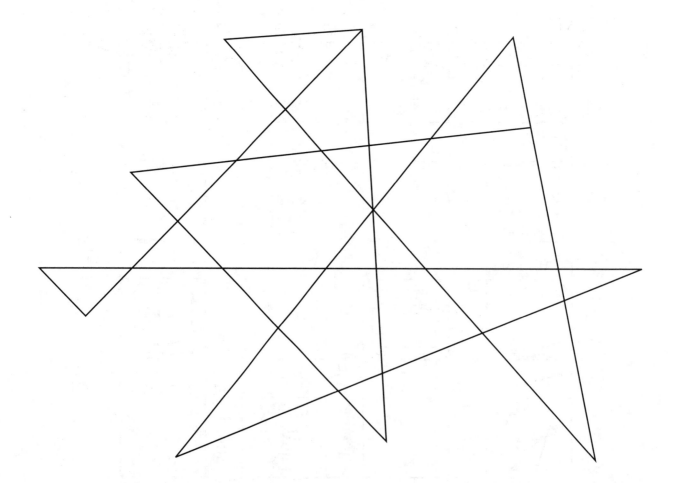

Picture Perfect

43

Circle these things: a mermaid, a treasure chest, a dolphin, and a crab.

Spun Shapes

44

Circle the shape that is not like the others.

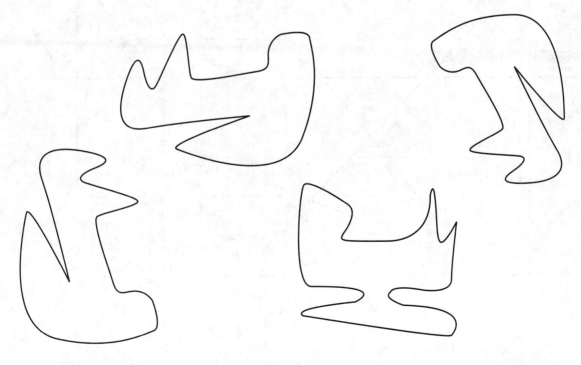

Map Madness!

45

Do you see Pedro? He is lost again! Follow the directions to get him back on track. Mark his ending spot with an **X**.

Directions:

1. Go east on Denny Way.

2. Go south on Olive St.

3. **END** End at the corner of Broadway.

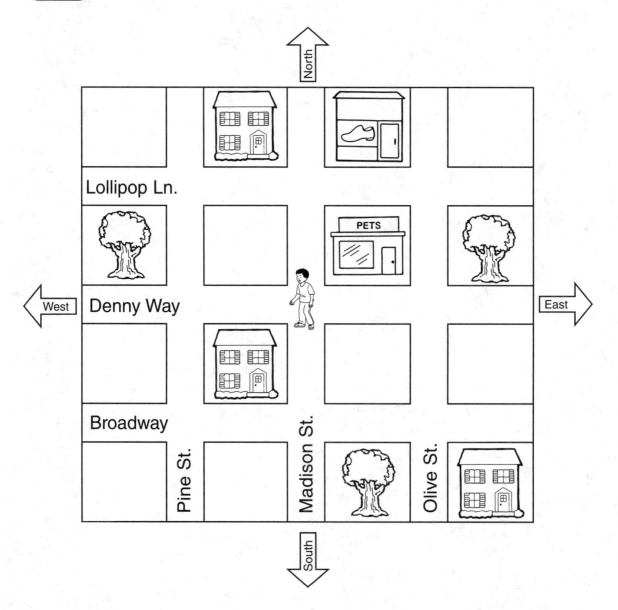

Missing Letter

46

The letter "e" has been taken out of the front, middle, or end of these words. The letter might be used twice. What are the words?

yllow: _____   blu: _____

grn: _____   rd: _____

Letter Scramble

47

Make two words using all of these letters: tna. Then look at the picture, and color one of the words you find.

1. _____

2. _____

Word Circles

48

Start at any letter. Go left or right. What foods can you spell? Write them in the circles.

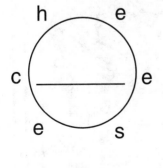

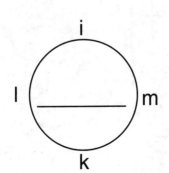

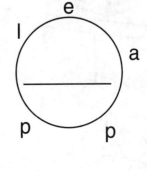

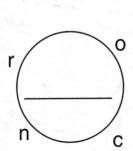

Transformers

49

Change one letter at a time to get from the top word to the bottom word. Each row must make a real word.

Example:

p	a	n
p	**i**	n
p	i	**g**
b	i	g

b	o	y
t	a	p

Colorful Foods

50

Can you find six foods that begin with the letter "b"? Color your answers.

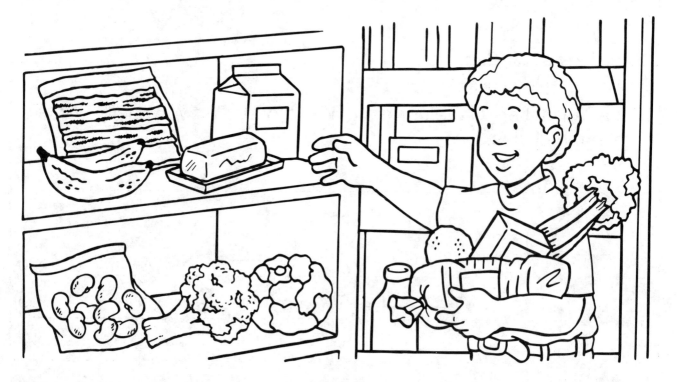

34 ©*Teacher Created Resources, Inc.*

Fronts and Backs

51

Directions:

1. These letters are the "fronts" and "backs" of words.
2. Find a partner. Make a word using the "fronts" and "backs" provided. Write it in your space.
3. Take turns writing words.
4. If you cannot make a new word, you are out.
5. The person with the most words wins!

Fronts	Backs
ca	rd
sta	rt
ho	me
stri	ge
co	ke
	pe

Player #1	Player #2

Hide and Seek

52

Can you find the two animals hiding in this sentence? Circle them.

Example: Help igloos!

Alec owned ogres.

Crossword

53

Read the clues and fill in the letters.

Across

1. You are able to do something.
4. how old you are
5. For tic-tac-toe, you need three in a _____.

Down

1. an automobile
2. It happened long _____.
3. The opposite of *old* is _____ .

1	2	3
4	*g*	
5		

Missing Letter

54

The letter "a" has been taken out of the front, middle, or end of these words. What are the words?

ct: _____ , _____   nt: _____

rt: _____ , _____   bg: _____

mp: _____

Hide and Seek

55

Can you find the three animals hiding in this sentence? Circle them.

Example: Help ig⟨loos!⟩

Do goats pant?

Transformers

56

Change one letter at a time to get from the top word to the bottom word. Each row must make a real word.

Example:

p	a	n
p	**i**	n
p	i	**g**
b	i	g

h	a	t
b	e	d

Word Circles

57

Start at any letter. Go left or right. What toys can you spell? Write them in the circles.

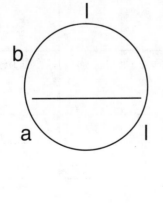

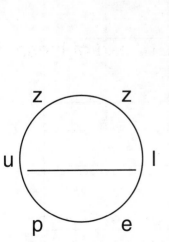

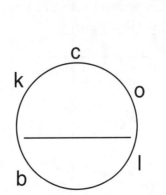

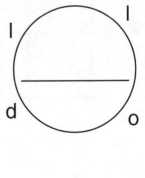

Crossword Challenge

58

Directions:

1. Using different-colored pens, work with a partner to put these words into the crossword puzzle. Each word must touch at least one other word.
2. Now, take turns adding new words to the puzzle. Be creative!
3. The person who can add the most new words wins.

stand   **ten**   bald   **end**

		S	T	A	R	T		

Missing Letter

59

The letter "o" has been taken out of the front, middle, or end of these words. The letter might be used twice. What are the words?

bw: _____   hp: _____

z: _____   yu: _____

cw: _____   ne: _____

wn: _____ , _____

Help Mr. Mallard

60

Mr. Mallard is at the grocery store. He can only buy things that start with the letter "c." Can you find five things that he can buy? Circle them.

Transformers

61

Change one letter at a time to get from the top word to the bottom word. Each row must make a real word.

Example:

p	a	n
p	**i**	n
p	i	**g**
b	i	g

c	a	t
d	o	g

Letter Scramble

62

Make two words using all of these letters: lwo. Then look at the picture, and color one of the words you find.

1. _____   2. _____

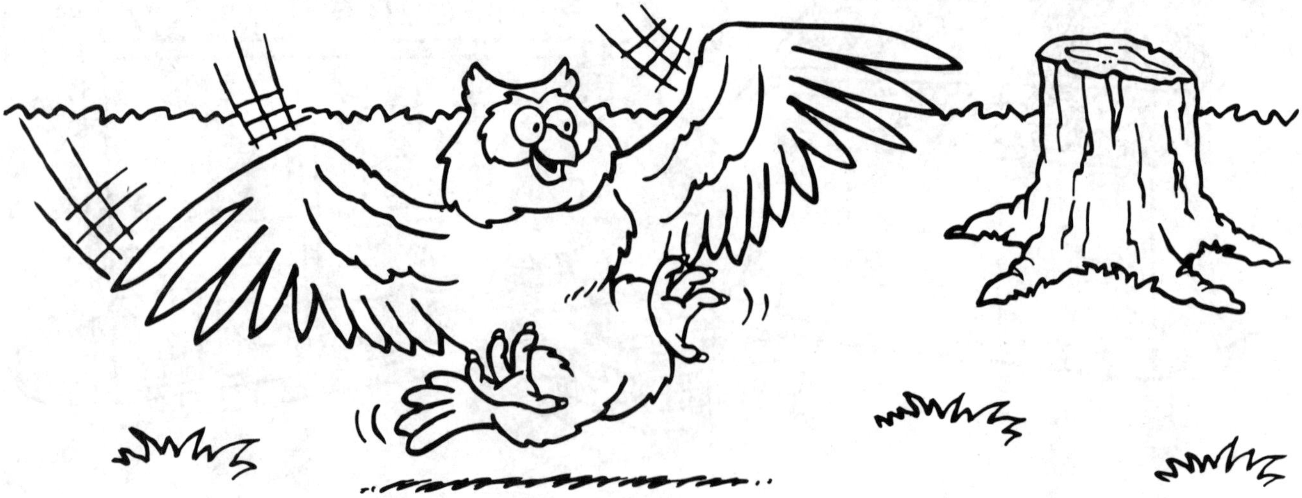

Crossword

63

Read the clues and fill in the letters.

Across

1. able to

4. My twin sister is the same _____.

5. not a column, but a _____

Down

1. My mom drives a _____.

2. It happened long _____.

3. Do you want an old toy or a _____ one?

1	2	3
4		
5 r		

Word Circles

64

Start at any letter. Go left or right. What animals can you spell? Write them in the circles.

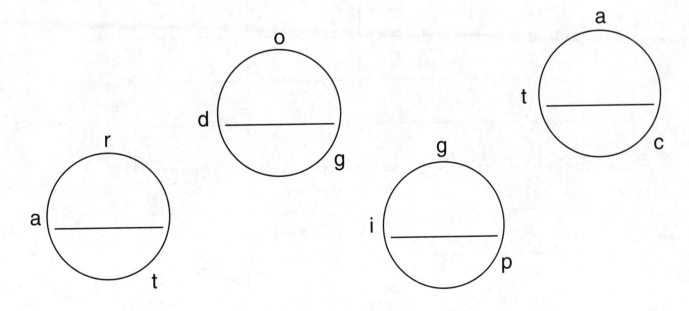

Changing Letters

65

Directions:

1. Find a partner. Start with the word below.

2. Change one letter to make a new word. Write this word in the next row.

3. Take turns. You can't use a word more than once.

4. If you cannot make a new word, you are out. When you reach the end of the puzzle together, you both win!

Example:

p	a	n
p	**i**	n
p	i	**g**
b	i	g

Start	c	a	t
1.			
2.			
3.			
4.			
5.			
6.			
7.			
8.			
9.			
10.			

42 ©Teacher Created Resources, Inc.

Colorful Foods

66

Can you find six foods that begin with the letter "p"? Color your answers.

Transformers

67

Change one letter at a time to get from the top word to the bottom word. Each row must make a real word.

Example:

p	a	n
p	**i**	n
p	i	**g**
b	i	g

h	o	t
p	a	d

Crack the Code

68

What travels around the world but stays in the corner? Crack the code to find out!

m	s	a	t	p
1	2	3	4	5

	■					
3		2	4	3	1	5

Word Circles

69

Start at any letter. Go left or right. What school supplies can you spell? Write them in the circles.

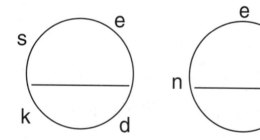
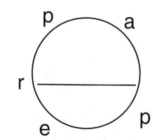
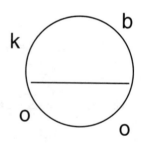

Letter Scramble

70

Make two words using all of these letters: pti. Then look at the picture, and color one of the words you find.

1. _____

2. _____

Scrambled Words

71

What words can you make using these letters?

gpi: _____   atc: _____ , _____

taf: _____   bda: _____ , _____

Transformers

72

Change one letter at a time to get from the top word to the bottom word. Each row must make a real word.

Example:

p	a	n
p	i	n
p	i	g
b	i	g

t	o	p
h	a	t

Crossword

73

Read the clues and fill in the letters.

Across

1. _____ Newtons® are a type of cookie.
4. number one, in cards
5. You use it to catch butterflies.

Down

1. It blows air.
2. _____ cream
3. to buy

1	2	3
4		e
5		

Beginnings and Ends Game

Directions:

1. Find a partner.

2. Look at the pictures below. Think of the words they show.

3. Start at *cat*. This word ends with the letter "t." Which word begins with the letter "t"? The first one has been done for you.

4. Take turns drawing lines to the next picture. Also, write the words you use.

5. If you cannot find a word in one minute, your partner wins. If you can use every picture, you both win!

cat

top

Letter Scramble

75

Make two words using all of these letters: npa. Then look at the picture, and color the words you find.

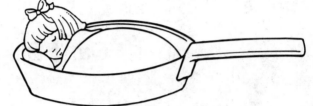

1. _____

2. _____

Word Circles

76

Start at any letter. Go left or right. What animals can you spell? Write them in the circles.

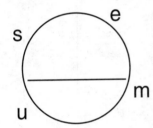 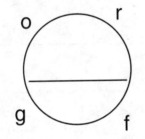 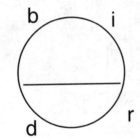 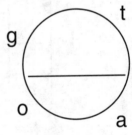

Missing Letter

77

The letter "i" has been taken out of the front, middle, or end of these words. What are the words?

ar: _____   ce: _____

hm: _____   sk: _____

nk: _____   st: _____

pt: _____   wn: _____

pn: _____

Hide and Seek

78

Can you find the two animals hiding in this sentence? Circle them.

Example: Hel**p ig**loos!

Can't Bill go at all?

Transformers

79

Change one letter at a time to get from the top word to the bottom word. Each row must make a real word.

Example:

p	a	n
p	i	n
p	i	**g**
b	i	g

m	o	p
c	a	r

Colorful Animals

80

Can you find three animals that begin with the letter "g"? Color your answers.

Crack the Code

81

What runs but never walks? Crack the code to find out!

e	w	r	t	a
1	2	3	4	5

2	5	4	1	3

Word Circles

82

Start at any letter. Go left or right. What colors can you spell? Write them in the circles.

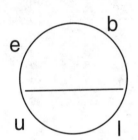 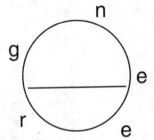 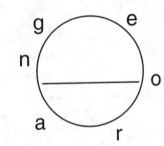 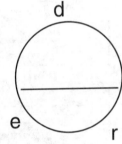

Crossword

83

Read the clues and fill in the letters.

Across

1. a small house

4. Three minus two equals _____.

5. The opposite of *lost* is _____.

Down

1. _____ are you feeling today?

2. one, in Spanish

3. eight, nine, _____, eleven

1	2	3
	u	
4		
5		

Word Puzzles

Rhyme Game

84

Directions:

1. Find a partner. Each player should use a different-colored pen. Then, look at the words below.

2. Race your partner to write rhymes for these words.

3. Once you write a rhyme in a box, the box is closed.

4. Whoever closes the most boxes wins!

car	**cat**	**dog**
rhyme	rhyme	rhyme
ring	**big**	**lost**
rhyme	rhyme	rhyme
top	**hill**	**best**
rhyme	rhyme	rhyme

Crossword

85

Read the clues and fill in the letters.

Across

1. something you might chew
4. short way to say United States of America
5. Have you cleaned your room _____ ?

Down

1. a man
2. _____ a hammer to pound nails.
3. a welcome _____

1	2	3
4		
5 Y		

Letter Scramble

86

Make two words using all of these letters: ugm. Then look at the picture, and color the words you find.

1. _____

2. _____

©Teacher Created Resources, Inc.

Word Circles

87

Start at any letter. Go left or right. What clothes can you spell? Write them in the circles.

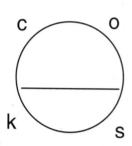
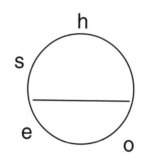
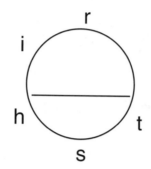
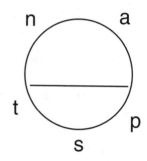

Hide and Seek

88

Can you find the two animals hiding in this sentence? Circle them.

Example: Help igloos!

Be earlier at once!

Transformers

89

Change one letter at a time to get from the top word to the bottom word. Each row must make a real word.

Example:

p	a	n
p	**i**	n
p	i	**g**
b	i	g

t	r	y
b	o	w

Hide and Seek

90

Can you find the five animals hiding in this sentence? Circle them.

Example: Help igloos!

If Rogers wants nails, it will be easy.

Missing Letter

91

The letter "p" has been taken out of the front, middle, or end of these words. The letter might be used twice. What are the words?

lug: _____   ond: _____

an: _____   tri: _____

dro: _____   um: _____

ae: _____

Crossword

92

Read the clues and fill in the letters.

Across

  1. short way to say "In my opinion"
  4. Tomato sauce comes in a
    tin _____.
  5. what you use to see

Down

  1. When you bump your head,
    you need _____ .
  2. April, _____ , June, July
  3. a single thing

1 i	2	3
4		
5		

Crossword Challenge

93

Directions:

1. Using different-colored pens, work with a partner to put these words into the crossword puzzle. Each word must touch at least one other word.

2. Now, take turns adding new words to the puzzle. Be creative!

3. The person who can add the most words wins.

tent	**frog**	noon	**mini**

				E				
				N				
				D				
				I				
				N				
				G				

 ©*Teacher Created Resources, Inc.*

Missing Letter

94

The letter "u" has been taken out of the front, middle, or end of these words. What are the words?

bs: _____   mg: _____

gm: _____   yo: _____

cp: _____   rn: _____

se: _____   tg: _____

hg: _____

Help Mr. Mallard

95

Mr. Mallard is packing to go on a trip. He can only take things that can be spelled with three letters. Can you find at least nine things he can pack? Circle them.

Crossword

96

Read the clues and fill in the letters.

Across

1. Baked beans come in a _____ can.

4. one, in cards

5. In the winter, it's easy to _____ cold.

Down

1. a popular playground game

2. frozen water

3. The fish was caught in a _____.

1	2	3
4 a		
5		

Letter Scramble

97

Make two words using all of these letters: ent. Then look at the picture, and color the words you find.

1. _____   2. _____

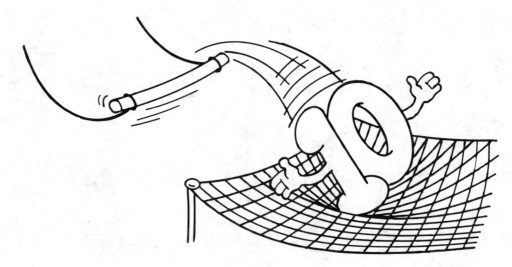

56   ©*Teacher Created Resources, Inc.*

Hide and Seek

98

Can you find the two animals hiding in this sentence? Circle them.

Example: Help igloos!

Elvis lugs nails.

Missing Letter

99

The letter "t" has been taken out of the front, middle, or end of these words. The letter might be used twice. What are the words?

ae: _____   ea: _____ , _____

he: _____   an: _____ , _____

ca: _____   ar: _____ , _____

op: _____

Colorful Foods

100

Can you find five foods that begin with the letter "s"?   Color your answers.

Fronts and Backs

101

Directions:

1. These letters are the "fronts" and "backs" of words.
2. Find a partner. Make a word using the "fronts" and "backs" provided. Write it in your space.
3. Take turns writing words.
4. If you cannot make a new word, you are out.
5. The person with the most words wins!

Fronts	Backs
wi	nd
be	lt
frie	st
ba	ast
ha	
le	
po	
wa	
fe	

Player #1	Player #2

Word Puzzles

Letter Scramble
102

Make two words using all of these letters: tpo. Then look at the picture, and color the words you find.

1. _____   2. _____

Crossword
103

Read the clues and fill in the letters.

Across

1. angry

4. It happened a long time _____.

5. It hangs from a basketball hoop.

Down

1. a male human

2. My best friend is the same _____ as I am.

3. a small, round mark

1	2	3
4		O
5		

Hide and Seek

104

Can you find the three animals hiding in this sentence? Circle them.

Example: Help igloos!

Catherine uses nails to add pictures.

Missing Letter

105

The letter "b" has been taken out of the front, middle, or end of these words. The letter might be used twice. What are the words?

at: _____   ook: _____

ump: _____   su: _____

we: _____   ug: _____

ull: _____   ul: _____

Transformers

106

Change one letter at a time to get from the top word to the bottom word. Each row must make a real word.

Example:

p	a	n
p	**i**	n
p	i	**g**
b	i	g

b	i	g
h	a	t

107 Number Ladder

Climb the ladder to fill in the missing number.

19
16
13
7
4

108 Math Path

Pick the best starting number, and then go up/down or left/right until you have touched all of the spaces once.

What is the *highest* total you can end with? Draw your path. **Total:** _____

3	–	2
+	6	

109 Math Triangle

Fill in the blank boxes so that the sum of each side of the triangle is seven.

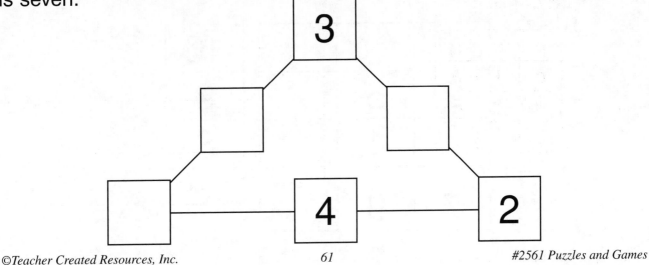

Fill in the Blanks

110

Fill in the blank to make this equation true.

$$\begin{array}{r} 1\,\square \\ +\quad 9 \\ \hline 2\ 4 \end{array}$$

Thinking of a Number

111

I am thinking of a three-digit number.

- The first digit is two more than the second.
- The last digit is three more than the first.

	2	

In Addition

112

Fill in the blanks with the numbers 1–9 so that the sum of each row is the number to the right, and the sum of each column is the number below it.

1		6	10
2	5	2	9
	1	3	8

7	9	11

62   ©*Teacher Created Resources, Inc.*

Thinking of a Number

I am thinking of a three-digit number.

- The third digit is two more than the first.
- The sum of all the digits is fifteen.

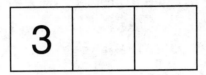

Math Path

114

Pick the best starting number, and then go up/down or left/right until you have touched all of the spaces once. What is the *highest* total you can end with? Draw your path.

1	+	3	–	1

–

3	**Total:** _____

Sudoku

115

Each row and column has the numbers 1, 2, and 3. Fill in the blanks to complete the puzzle.

		3
	3	
3		2

Addition Challenge

116

Directions:

1. Pick a colored pen. Have your partner pick a different color.
2. One player is on the left, and one player is on the right.
3. Look at the numbers in the middle. In each row, circle the numbers on your side that add up to the number in the middle. You can circle as many numbers as you need. For example:

1	2	3	4	5	⑥	7	⑧	⑨	**23**	9	8	7	6	5	4	3	2	1

4. Once you have circled any combination of numbers, put an **X** on the number in the middle. That row is now closed. You get a point for each **X**.
5. Start at the same time, and solve as many rows as you can before your partner.
6. You do not have to solve the rows in order. (You can start at the end or skip around.)
7. At the end, the person with the most points wins.

Player #1										Player #2								
1	2	3	4	5	6	7	8	9	**25**	9	8	7	6	5	4	3	2	1
1	2	3	4	5	6	7	8	9	**13**	9	8	7	6	5	4	3	2	1
1	2	3	4	5	6	7	8	9	**19**	9	8	7	6	5	4	3	2	1
1	2	3	4	5	6	7	8	9	**15**	9	8	7	6	5	4	3	2	1
1	2	3	4	5	6	7	8	9	**22**	9	8	7	6	5	4	3	2	1
1	2	3	4	5	6	7	8	9	**11**	9	8	7	6	5	4	3	2	1
1	2	3	4	5	6	7	8	9	**10**	9	8	7	6	5	4	3	2	1

Sudoku

117

Each row and column has the numbers 1, 2, and 3. Fill in the blanks to complete the puzzle.

2		3
	3	
	2	1

Math Path

118

Pick the best starting number, and then go up/down or left/right until you have touched all of the spaces once. What is the *highest* total you can end with? Draw your path.

4	–	2
+	1	

Total : _____

Number Ladder

119

Climb the ladder to fill in the missing number.

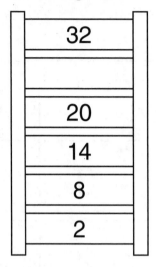

Thinking of a Number

120

I am thinking of a three-digit number.

- Each digit is three more than the one before it.

	4	

Sudoku

121

Each row and column has the numbers 1, 2, and 3. Fill in the blanks to complete the puzzle.

	1	
1	2	
		1

In Addition

Fill in the blanks with the numbers 1–9 so that the sum of each row is the number to the right, and the sum of each column is the number below it.

	1	3	13
1		4	11
8		9	23
18	13	16	

Math Path

Pick the best starting number, and then go up/down or left/right until you have touched all of the spaces once. What is the *highest* total you can end with? Draw your path.

3	–	1
–	8	

Total : _____

Tic-Tac-Toe Race

124

Directions:

Example:

1. Pick a colored pen. Have your partner pick a different color.

2. Choose a tic-tac-toe board, and sit side by side.

3. Start at the same time, and race to solve the math problems.

4. When you solve a problem, write the answer in the box.

5. If you get three in a row, you win.

6. Check your answers. If your partner wrote a wrong answer, the space is yours!

2 + 5	4 + 2	8 + 3
9 + 5 14	4 + 5	2 + 7
1 + 6	3 + 9	5 + 7

Game Boards:

3 + 2	5 + 4	9 + 2
7 + 4	3 + 9	1 + 7
6 + 8	9 + 7	8 + 7

3 + 8	4 + 2	9 + 4
7 + 9	1 + 6	5 + 6
8 + 4	5 + 3	7 + 3

4 + 5	2 + 9	8 + 1
3 + 7	6 + 4	8 + 7
5 + 7	8 + 3	2 + 6

5 + 5	9 + 9	8 + 8
7 + 7	6 + 6	3 + 3
2 + 2	4 + 4	1 + 1

Fill in the Blanks

125

Fill in the blanks to make this equation true.

$$\begin{array}{r} \boxed{} \\ +\ \ 6 \\ \hline \boxed{}\ 4 \end{array}$$

Thinking of a Number

126

I am thinking of a three-digit number.

• The third digit is the sum of the first two digits.

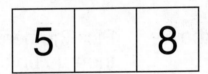

Math Triangle

127

Fill in the blanks so that the sum of each side of the triangle is ten.

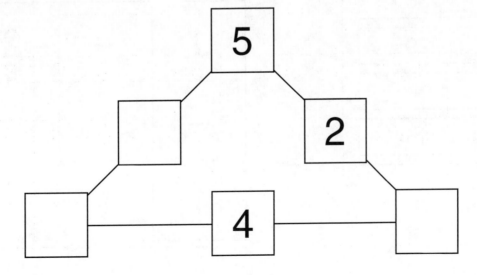

In Addition
128

Fill in the blanks with the numbers 1–9 so that the sum of each row is the number to the right, and the sum of each column is the number below it.

8		3	**13**
			3
	2	9	**15**
13	**5**	**13**	

Number Ladder
129

Climb the ladder to fill in the missing number.

43
36
29
15
8

Math Path
130

Pick the best starting number, and then go up/down or left/right until you have touched all of the spaces once. What is the *highest* total you can end with? Draw your path.

Total: _____

1	–	2
–	1	
1	+	

Sudoku
131

Each row and column has the numbers 1, 2, and 3. Fill in the blanks to complete the puzzle.

1		2
	1	
	2	

Math Triangle
132

Fill in the blanks so that the sum of each side of the triangle is five.

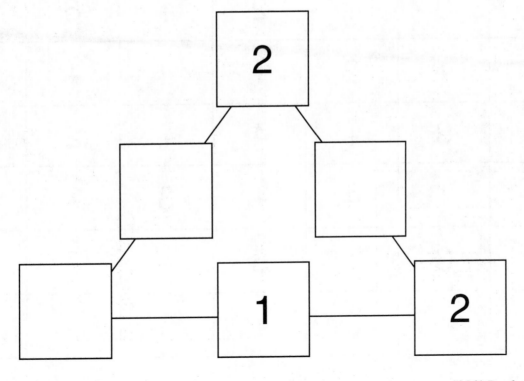

Snake Race

Directions:

1. Find a partner. Each player should use a different-colored pen.

2. Sit side by side, and put the game board in front of you.

3. Look for snakes that add up to thirteen. The numbers have to be touching. (You cannot jump around.) Once a number is taken, you cannot use it again.

4. Take turns. You have 30 seconds to find a snake.

5. If you cannot find a snake in 30 seconds, the other person wins.

Example:

5	+	4	+
+	3	+	4
7	+	6	+
+	3	+	8

Game Board:

8	+	4	+	1	+	5
+	3	+	2	+	6	+
5	+	2	+	4	+	3
+	9	+	4	+	2	+
6	+	4	+	3	+	5
+	3	+	5	+	7	+
7	+	3	+	3	+	2

 ©*Teacher Created Resources, Inc.*

Sudoku
134

Each row and column has the numbers 1, 2, and 3. Fill in the blanks to complete the puzzle.

1		
	3	1
	1	

In Addition
135

Fill in the blanks with the numbers 1–9 so that the sum of each row is the number to the right, and the sum of each column is the number below it.

	2		13
3		9	18
6		1	14
13	15	17	

Thinking of a Number

136

I am thinking of a three-digit number.

- The first digit is three more than the second digit.
- The last digit is four more than the second digit.

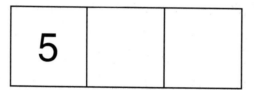

Number Ladder

137

Climb the ladder to fill in the missing number.

46
37
19
10
1

Math Path

138

Pick the best starting number, and then go up/down or left/right until you have touched all of the spaces once. What is the *highest* total you can end with? Draw your path.

Total: _____

3	–	1
–	6	
2	+	

74

©*Teacher Created Resources, Inc.*

Plus or Minus Game

139

Directions:

1. Find a partner. Each of you will need a copy of this sheet and a different-colored pen.

2. Look at the rows below. In each row, you have to add or subtract to get from the first number to the last. The first one has been done for you.

3. Race your partner to solve the rows. You do not have to go in order. The person who solves the most rows wins.

4. Ready, set, go!

8	+ or ⊖	3	⊕ or −	2	=	7
9	+ or −	6	+ or −	1	=	2
6	+ or −	3	+ or −	7	=	2
5	+ or −	4	+ or −	2	=	3
10	+ or −	9	+ or −	6	=	7
14	+ or −	6	+ or −	4	=	4
8	+ or −	4	+ or −	3	=	9

Sudoku

140

Each row and column has the numbers 1, 2, and 3. Fill in the blanks to complete the puzzle.

2	3	
1	2	

Math Triangle

141

Fill in the blanks so that the sum of each side of the triangle is eight.

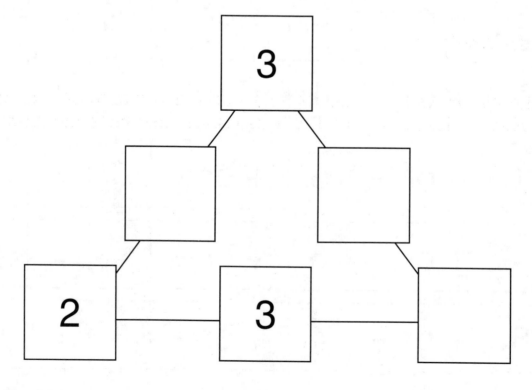

76

©*Teacher Created Resources, Inc.*

142 Fill in the Blanks

Fill in the blanks to make this equation true.

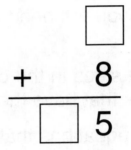

$$\begin{array}{r} \square \\ +\quad 8 \\ \hline \square\ 5 \end{array}$$

143 Sudoku

Each row and column has the numbers 1, 2, and 3. Fill in the blanks to complete the puzzle.

1	2	
2		1

144 In Addition

Fill in the blanks with the numbers 1–9 so that the sum of each row is the number to the right, and the sum of each column is the number below it.

			11
2	5		15
	4	3	8
6	15	13	

Meet Your Match

145

Directions:

1. Find a partner. Each of you will need a copy of this sheet and a different-colored pen.

2. Look at the left and right sides in the columns below. On each side, there are equations that have the same answer.

3. Draw lines between the equations that have the same answer.

4. The person who can draw the most lines wins.

2 + 2	6 + 6
3 + 10	1 + 3
4 + 5	2 + 9
2 + 4	4 + 4
3 + 2	4 + 1
3 + 9	6 + 7
7 + 3	3 + 6
3 + 4	2 + 5
5 + 6	6 + 4
2 + 6	3 + 3

Sudoku
146

Each row and column has the numbers 1, 2, and 3. Fill in the blanks to complete the puzzle.

1		3
	1	
		1

Number Ladder
147

Climb the ladder to fill in the missing number.

58
47
25
14
3

Math Path
148

Pick the best starting number, and then go up/down or left/right until you have touched all of the spaces once. What is the *highest* total you can end with? Draw your path.

Total: _____

4	–	2
+	2	
3	–	

149 Math Triangle

Fill in the blanks so that the sum of each side of the triangle is fifteen.

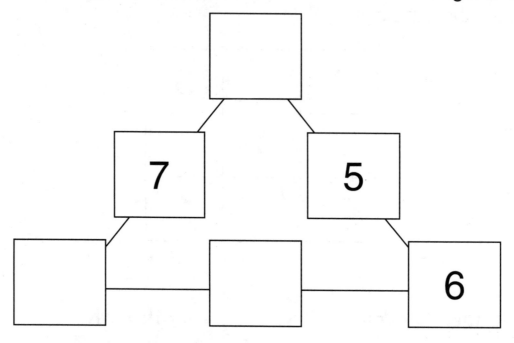

150 In Addition

Fill in the blanks with the numbers 1–9 so that the sum of each row is the number to the right, and the sum of each column is the number below it.

5	2		9
		5	9
1			9
8	7	12	

Snake Race

151

Directions:

1. Find a partner. Each player should use a different-colored pen.

2. Sit side by side, and put the game board in front of you.

3. Look for snakes that add up to seventeen. The numbers have to be touching. (You cannot jump around.) Once a number is taken, you cannot use it again.

4. Take turns. You have 30 seconds to find a snake.

5. If you cannot find a snake in 30 seconds, the other person wins.

Example:

5	+	4	+
+	5	+	8
7	+	6	+
+	5	+	3

Game Board:

4	+	5	+	5	+	6
+	3	+	2	+	7	+
5	+	6	+	3	+	3
+	8	+	4	+	6	+
9	+	4	+	2	+	1
+	2	+	6	+	7	+
4	+	3	+	5	+	4

Addition Challenge

152

Directions:

1. Pick a colored pen. Have your partner pick a different color.
2. One player is on the left, and one player is on the right.
3. Look at the numbers in the middle. In each row, circle the numbers on your side that add up to the number in the middle. You can circle as many numbers as you need. For example:

1	2	3	4	5	6	7	8	9	**23**	9	8	7	6	5	4	3	2	1

4. Once you have circled any combination of numbers, put an **X** on the number in the middle. That row is now closed. You get a point for each **X**.
5. Start at the same time, and solve as many rows as you can before your partner.
6. You do not have to solve the rows in order. (You can start at the end or skip around.)
7. At the end, the person with the most points wins.

Player #1										Player #2								
1	2	3	4	5	6	7	8	9	**27**	9	8	7	6	5	4	3	2	1
1	2	3	4	5	6	7	8	9	**15**	9	8	7	6	5	4	3	2	1
1	2	3	4	5	6	7	8	9	**18**	9	8	7	6	5	4	3	2	1
1	2	3	4	5	6	7	8	9	**32**	9	8	7	6	5	4	3	2	1
1	2	3	4	5	6	7	8	9	**40**	9	8	7	6	5	4	3	2	1
1	2	3	4	5	6	7	8	9	**31**	9	8	7	6	5	4	3	2	1
1	2	3	4	5	6	7	8	9	**17**	9	8	7	6	5	4	3	2	1

Alison's Notebook

153

Alison lost her notebook. Can you help her find it? Circle the correct notebook.

Here are facts about Alison's notebook:

> ✔ It has spiral binding.
>
> ✔ It does not have a star on it.
>
> ✔ It does not have stripes on it.

Odd Animal Out

154

Circle the animal that does not belong.

Why doesn't it belong? _____

What's Next?

155

Draw the shape that should come next.

[square] [circle] [circle] [square] [circle] [circle] ____

Add One Or Two

156

Directions:

1. Find a partner. Each player should use a different-colored pen.
2. Look at the boxes below.
3. Take turns coloring in boxes.
4. You can color in either one or two boxes per turn.
5. Whoever colors in the last box wins.

Example:

Game Boards:

1.

2.

3.

4.

Odd Animal Out

157

Circle the animal that does not belong.

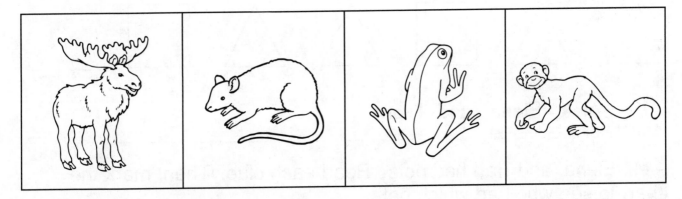

Why doesn't it belong? _____

Logic Maze

158

Move up/down or left/right (not diagonal) to a space that has one of the same symbols as the box you are in.

Example:

159 What's Next?

Draw the shape that should come next.

      ___

160 Alek, Elena, and Tran

Alek, Elena, and Tran had pets. Read each clue. Then, mark the chart to see who had which pet.

Clues:

✓ Tran did not have the cat or the pig.

✓ Elena did not have the pig.

Example:

	Walk	Run	Jump
Mary		X	X
Seth	X	X	
Rich	X		X

Chart:

	Cat	Dog	Pig
Alek			
Elena			
Tran			

Answers:

Which pet did Alek have? _____

Which pet did Elena have? _____

Which pet did Tran have? _____

Lisa's Sock

161

Lisa lost one of her socks. Can you help her find it? Circle the correct sock. Here are facts about Lisa's sock:

| ✓ It has polka dots on it.
| ✓ It does not have lightning bolts on it.
| ✓ It does not have stars on it.

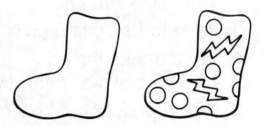

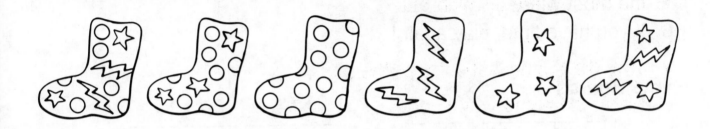

Odd Animal Out

162

Circle the animal that does not belong.

Why doesn't it belong? _____

Three-in-a-Row

163

Directions:

1. Find a partner.
2. Choose **X**s or **O**s.
3. Take turns putting an **X** or an **O** in a box.
4. Try to make three in a row, either up-and-down or right-and-left (no diagonals).
5. At the end, count how many three-in-a-rows you made. The person who makes the most wins.
6. If you have time, play again!

Example:

X	X	X	O
O	X	X	X
O	O	X	X
O	O	O	O

Game Boards:

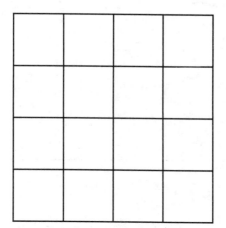
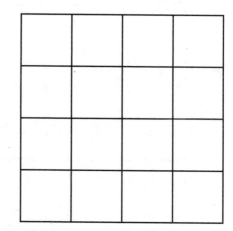
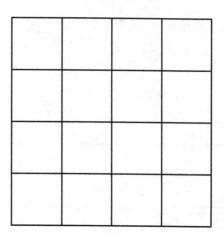
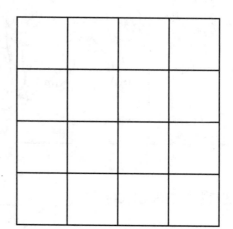

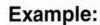

Odd Animal Out

164

Circle the animal that does not belong.

Why doesn't it belong? _____

Logic Maze

165

Move up/down or left/right (not diagonal) to a space that has one of the same symbols as the box you are in.

Example:

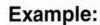

Alek, Elena, and Tran

166

Alek, Elena, and Tran ran a race. Read each clue. Then, mark the chart to see how they finished.

Clues:

✓ Elena was faster that Alek.

✓ Tran won the race.

Example:

	Walk	Run	Jump
Mary		X	X
Seth	X	X	
Rich	X		X

Chart:

	1st	2nd	3rd
Alek			
Elena			
Tran			

Answers:

How did Alek finish the race? _____

How did Elena finish the race? _____

How did Tran finish the race? _____

Boxed Out

Directions:

Example:

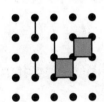

1. Find a partner. Each player should use a different-colored pen.

2. Look at the dots below.

3. Take turns drawing a short line between two dots.

4. Try to make closed boxes. When you make a box, color it in. Then, go again.

5. The person who makes the most boxes wins.

Game Board:

Alek, Elena, and Tran

Alek, Elena, and Tran ate lunch. Read each clue. Then, mark the chart to see who ate what.

Clues:

✓ Tran did not eat a sandwich.

✓ Elena did not eat a hot dog.

✓ Alek had the salad.

Example:

	Walk	Run	Jump
Mary		X	X
Seth	X	X	
Rich	X		X

Chart:

	Sandwich	Hot Dog	Salad
Alek			
Elena			
Tran			

Answers:

What did Alek eat for lunch? _____

What did Elena eat for lunch? _____

What did Tran eat for lunch? _____

 ©Teacher Created Resources, Inc.

Odd Animal Out

169

Circle the animal that does not belong.

Why doesn't it belong? _____

Logic Maze

170

Move up/down or left/right (not diagonal) to a space that has one of the same symbols as the box you are in.

Example:

Start △ □	◯ ☺	◯ ⬡	◯ △	□ △
△ ⬡	□ △	☺ ⬡	◯ ☺	□ ◯
☺ ⬡	⬡ □	□ ☺	⬡ △	□ ⬡
☺ □	◯ △	◯ ☺	△ □	☺ △
△ ⬡	□ ⬡	◯ □	□ ☺	Finish ☺ ◯

Four-in-a-Row

171

Directions:

1. Find a partner.
2. Choose **X**s or **O**s.
3. Take turns putting an **X** or an **O** in a box.
4. Try to make four in a row, either up-and-down or right-and-left (no diagonals).
5. At the end, count how many four-in-a-rows you made. The person who makes the most wins.
6. If you have time, play again!

Example:

X	X	X	X	O	X
O	X	X	X	X	X
O	O	X	X	O	X
X	O	X	O	O	O
O	O	O	O	X	O
X	O	O	O	O	X

Game Boards:

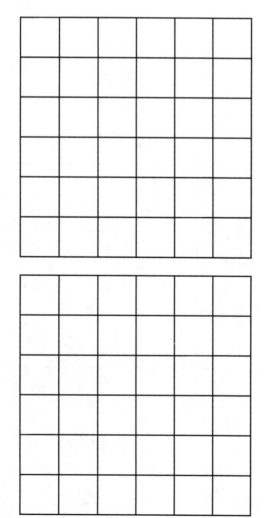

What's Next?

172

Draw the shape that should come next.

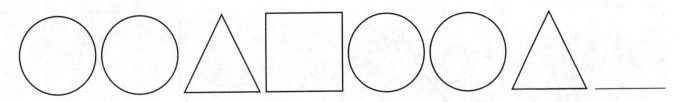

Dan's Kite

173

Dan lost his kite. Can you help him find it? Circle the correct kite.
Here are facts about Dan's kite:

> ✓ It has stripes on it.
>
> ✓ It does not have bows on it.
>
> ✓ It does not have flowers on it.

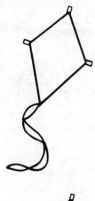

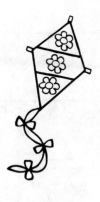
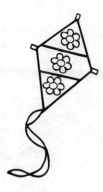

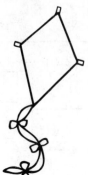

©*Teacher Created Resources, Inc.*

#2561 *Puzzles and Games*

Odd Animal Out

174

Circle the animal that does not belong.

Why doesn't it belong? _____

Logic Maze

175

Move up/down or left/right (not diagonal) to a space that has one of the same symbols as the box you are in.

Example:

Blocked

Directions:

1. Find a partner. Each player should use a different-colored pen.

2. Take turns drawing lines from one dot to another. You can draw only vertical (up and down) lines. Your partner can draw only horizontal (side to side) lines.

3. Once any line touches a dot, the dot is closed and cannot be used again.

4. The first person who cannot make a move loses.

Example:

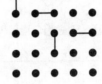

Game Board:

©*Teacher Created Resources, Inc.*

Mike's Snowman

Mike's snowman melted. Now he needs help building a new one. He wants it to look like the one that melted. Can you help him find it? Circle the correct snowman.

Here are facts about Mike's snowman:

✓ It had a carrot nose.
✓ It had four buttons.
✓ It had two branches for arms.

Odd Animal Out

Circle the animal that does not belong.

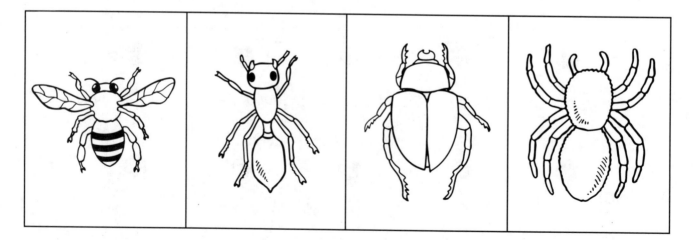

Why doesn't it belong? _____

What's Next?

179

Draw the shape that should come next.

☐ ☐ △ ☐ ____

Alek, Elena, and Tran

180

Alek, Elena, and Tran wore shirts. Read each clue. Then, mark the chart to see who wore which shirt.

Clues:

✓ Elena did not wear the striped shirt.

✓ Tran did not wear the plain shirt.

✓ Alek did not wear the striped shirt or the plain shirt.

Example:

	Walk	Run	Jump
Mary		✕	✕
Seth	✕	✕	
Rich	✕		✕

Chart:

	Striped Shirt	Plain Shirt	Dotted Shirt
Alek			
Elena			
Tran			

Answers:

What shirt did Alek wear? _____

What shirt did Elena wear? _____

What shirt did Tran wear? _____

181 What's Next?

Draw the shape that should come next.

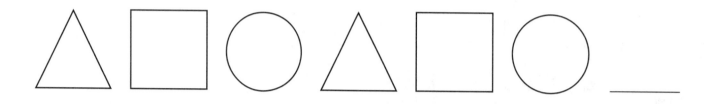

182 Tom's Pizza

Tom loves to eat pizza, but he always forgets what his favorite pizza looks like. Can you help him find it? Circle the correct pizza. Here are facts about Tom's pizza:

✓ Tom always orders pepperoni.
✓ Tom always orders mushrooms.
✓ Tom never orders onions.

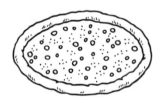 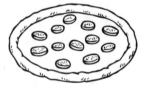 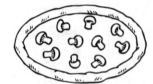 

  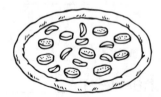 

Answer Key

Note: Answers are organized by puzzle number, not page number.

Picture Puzzles

1. seven things that do not belong: soccer ball, watch, train, skateboard, airplane, calculator, computer

2. The hippo with antlers is not a real animal.

4.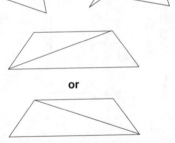

5.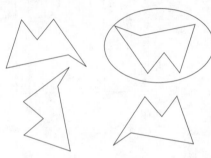

6. In the second picture, the hat is different, the cane is shorter, the jacket has no pocket, and the man has no ears or mustache.

7. The cat with webbed feet is not a real animal.

9.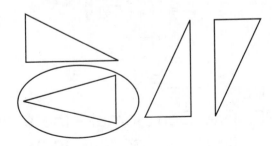

10.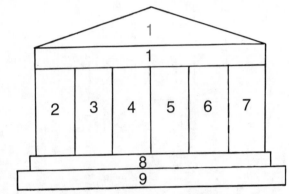

11. The horse with elephant ears is not a real animal.

12.

13.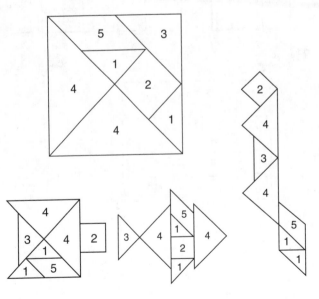

Answer Key *(cont.)*

14.

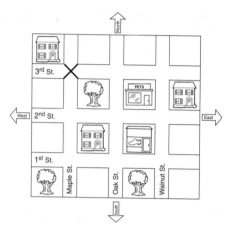

15.

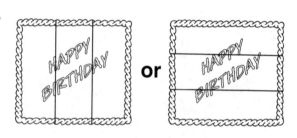

16. four

17.

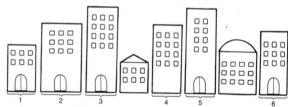

or

18.

19.

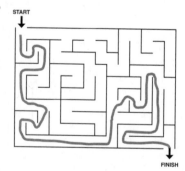

20.

21. In the second picture, there is one more bubble, the boy is wearing a friendship bracelet and a t-shirt with a lightning bolt on it, there is no sun out, and there is a cloud in the sky.

22.

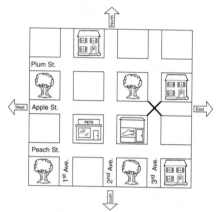

23.

24.

25.

26. five (Don't forget—the entire figure is a square, too!)

Answer Key *(cont.)*

27.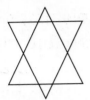

28. In the second picture, the crocodile is missing a front tooth, its tail is gone, one of its eyes has long eyelashes, there is a fish coming out of the water, and there is a rock.

29. Answers will vary but may be similar to:

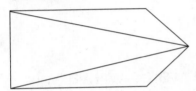

30. Answers will vary but may be similar to:

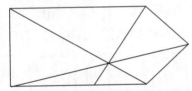

31. The squirrel with wings is not a real animal.

32. four

33.

34. three

35. six

37.

38.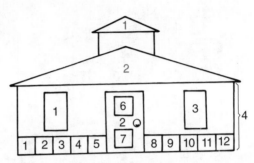

39. The cow with zebra stripes is not a real animal.

40. six things that do not belong: airplane, sunglasses, soccer ball, shoes, hot dog, book

41.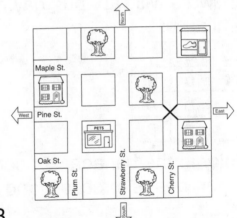

43.

44.

Answer Key (cont.)

45.

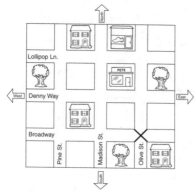

Word Puzzles

46. yellow, green, blue, red

47. ant, tan
    Color in the ant.

48. cheese, milk, apple, corn

49. Answers will vary but may be similar to:

b	o	y
t	**o**	**y**
t	**o**	**p**
t	a	p

50. Color in the bananas, bacon, butter, beans, broccoli, and bread.

51. Answers will vary but may include: card, cart, came, cage, cake, cape, start, stage, stake, home, hope, strike, stripe, cord, come, cope

52. Alec owned ogres.

53.

¹c	²a	³n
⁴a	g	e
⁵r	o	w

54. act and cat, rat and art, ant, bag, map

55. Do goats pant?

56. Answers will vary but may be similar to:

h	a	t
b	**a**	**t**
b	**a**	**d**
b	e	d

57. puzzle, ball, block, doll

58.

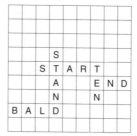

Other words will vary.

59. bow, zoo, cow, won and own, hop, you, one

60. Circle the corn, cookies, chips, crackers, and candy.

61. Answers will vary but may be similar to:

c	a	t
c	**o**	**t**
d	**o**	**t**
d	o	g

62. low, owl
    Color in the owl.

63.

¹c	²a	³n
⁴a	g	e
⁵r	o	w

Answer Key *(cont.)*

64. rat, dog, pig, cat

66. Color in the pears, plums, potatoes, pepperoni, pizza, and peas.

67. Answers will vary but may be similar to:

h	o	t
h	**a**	**t**
h	**a**	**d**
p	a	d

68. a stamp

69. desk, pen, paper, book

70. pit, tip
Color in the peach pit.

71. pig, fat, cat and act, bad and dab

72. Answers will vary but may be similar to:

t	o	p
h	**o**	**p**
h	**o**	**t**
h	a	t

73.

¹f	²i	³g
⁴a	c	e
⁵n	e	t

74. Order may vary.
cat→top→pen→
nest→table→ear→
rat→tiger→rock

75. pan, nap
Color the pan and the napping girl.

76. mouse, frog, bird, goat

77. air, him, ink, pit, pin, ice, ski, sit, win

78. Can't Bill go at all?

79. Answers will vary but may be similar to:

m	o	p
m	**a**	**p**
c	**a**	**p**
c	a	r

80. Color in the giraffe, the goat, and the gorilla.

81. water

82. blue, green, orange, red

83.

¹h	²u	³t
⁴o	n	e
⁵w	o	n

85.

¹g	²u	³m
⁴u	s	a
⁵y	e	t

86. gum, mug
Color in the gum and the mug.

87. sock, shoe, shirt, pants

Answer Key (cont.)

88. Be earlier at once!

89. Answers will vary but may be similar to:

t	r	y
t	**o**	**y**
b	**o**	**y**
b	o	w

90. If Rogers wants nails, it will be easy.

91. plug, pan, drop, ape, pond, trip, pump

92.

¹ i	² m	³ o
⁴ c	a	n
⁵ e	y	e

93.

				N				
				O				
				O				
		T	E	N	T			
				N				
				D				
		M	I	N	I			
				N				
	F	R	O	G				

Other words will vary.

94. bus, gum, cup, use, hug, mug, you, run, tug

95. Circle the hat, jar, lid, cat, pig, bat, box, pen, and top.

96.

¹ t	² i	³ n
⁴ a	c	e
⁵ g	e	t

97. net, ten
Color in the ten and the net.

98. Elvis lugs nails.

99. ate, the, cat, top, eat and tea, ant and tan, art and tar

100. Color in the salt, salad, sandwich, shrimp, and soup.

101. Answers will vary but may include: wind, wilt, bend, belt, best, beast, friend, band, hand, halt, lend, lest, least, pond, post, wand, fend, felt, feast

102. top, pot
Color in the pot and the lid (*top*).

103.

¹ m	² a	³ d
⁴ a	g	o
⁵ n	e	t

104. Catherine uses nails to add pictures.

105. bat, bump, web, bull, book, sub, bug, bulb

Answer Key (cont.)

106. Answers will vary but may be similar to:

b	i	g
b	**a**	**g**
b	**a**	**t**
h	a	t

Number Puzzles

107. 10

108. 7

Paths will vary but may be similar to:

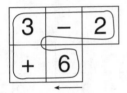

109.

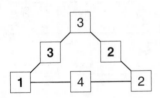

110.

$$\begin{array}{r} 1\boxed{5} \\ + 9 \\ \hline 2\,4 \end{array}$$

111.

4	2	**7**

112.

1	**3**	6
2	5	2
4	1	3

10
9
8

7	9	11

113.

3	**7**	5

114. 4

Paths will vary but may be similar to:

1	+	3	–	1
–				
3				

115.

1	**2**	3
2	3	1
3	**1**	2

116. Answers will vary but may be similar to:

Player #1										Player #2								
①2 3 4 5 6 ⑦⑧⑨									**25**	9⑧⑦6⑤4③②1								
1 2 3 4 5⑥⑦8 9									**13**	⑨8 7 6 5④3 2 1								
1②3 4 5 6 7⑧⑨									**19**	9 8⑦⑥⑤4 3 2①								
1 2 3 4 5 6⑦⑧9									**15**	9 8 7⑥⑤④3 2 1								
①②③4 5 6⑦8⑨									**22**	⑨8 7⑥⑤4 3②1								
1 2 3 4⑤⑥7 8 9									**11**	9 8 7 6⑤④3②1								
①2 3 4 5 6 7 8⑨									**10**	9 8 7 6 5④③②①								

117.

2	**1**	3
1	3	**2**
3	2	1

118. 3

Paths will vary but may be similar to:

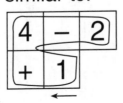

Answer Key *(cont.)*

119. 26

120.

1	4	7

121.

3	1	2
1	2	3
2	3	1

122.

9	1	3	13
1	6	4	11
8	6	9	23
18	13	16	

123. 4

Paths will vary but may be similar to:

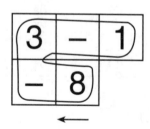

124.

3 + 2	5 + 4	9 + 2
5	9	11
7 + 4	3 + 9	1 + 7
11	12	8
6 + 8	9 + 7	8 + 7
14	16	15

3 + 8	4 + 2	9 + 4
11	6	13
7 + 9	1 + 6	5 + 6
16	7	11
8 + 4	5 + 3	7 + 3
12	8	10

4 + 5	2 + 9	8 + 1
9	11	9
3 + 7	6 + 4	8 + 7
10	10	15
5 + 7	8 + 3	2 + 6
12	11	8

5 + 5	9 + 9	8 + 8
10	18	16
7 + 7	6 + 6	3 + 3
14	12	6
2 + 2	4 + 4	1 + 1
4	8	2

125.

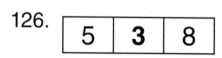
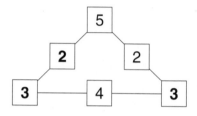

126.

5	3	8

127.

> 5
> 2   2
> 3   4   3

128.

8	2	3	13
1	1	1	3
4	2	9	15
13	5	13	

129. 22

130. 1

Paths will vary but may be similar to:

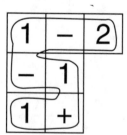

131.

1	3	2
2	1	3
3	2	1

Answer Key *(cont.)*

132.

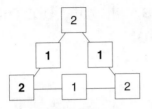

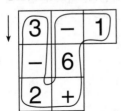

133. Answers will vary but may be similar to:

8	+	4	+	1	+	5
+	3	+	2	+	6	+
5	+	2	+	4	+	3
+	9	+	4	+	2	+
6	+	4	+	3	+	5
+	3	+	5	+	7	+
7	+	3	+	3	+	2

134.

1	**2**	**3**
2	3	1
3	1	**2**

135.

4	2	**7**	13
3	**6**	9	18
6	**7**	1	14
13	15	17	

136.

5	**2**	**6**

137. 28

138. 6

Paths will vary but may be similar to:

3	–	1
–	6	
2	+	

139.

8	+ or (−)	3	(+) or −	2	=	7
9	+ or (−)	6	+ or (−)	1	=	2
6	(+) or −	3	+ or (−)	7	=	2
5	+ or (−)	4	(+) or −	2	=	3
10	+ or (−)	9	(+) or −	6	=	7
14	+ or (−)	6	+ or (−)	4	=	4
8	(+) or −	4	+ or (−)	3	=	9

140.

2	3	**1**
1	2	**3**
3	**1**	**2**

141.

142.

$$\begin{array}{r} \boxed{7} \\ +\quad 8 \\ \hline \boxed{1}\,5 \end{array}$$

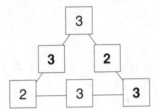

143.

1	2	**3**
2	**3**	1
3	**1**	**2**

144.

3	**6**	**2**	11
2	5	**8**	15
1	4	3	8
6	15	13	

Answer Key *(cont.)*

145.

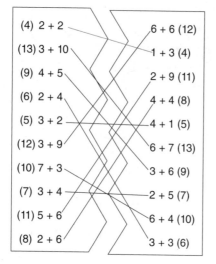

(4) 2 + 2   6 + 6 (12)
(13) 3 + 10   1 + 3 (4)
(9) 4 + 5   2 + 9 (11)
(6) 2 + 4   4 + 4 (8)
(5) 3 + 2   4 + 1 (5)
(12) 3 + 9   6 + 7 (13)
(10) 7 + 3   3 + 6 (9)
(7) 3 + 4   2 + 5 (7)
(11) 5 + 6   6 + 4 (10)
(8) 2 + 6   3 + 3 (6)

146.

1	**2**	3
3	1	**2**
2	3	1

147. 36

148. 3

Paths will vary but may be similar to:

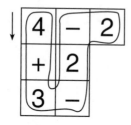

149.

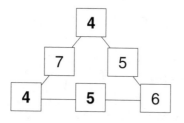

150.

5	2	**2**	9
2	2	5	9
1	**3**	5	9
8	7	12	

151. Answers will vary but may be similar to:

4	+	5	+	5	+	6
+	3	+	2	+	7	+
5	+	6	+	3	+	3
+	8	+	4	+	6	+
9	+	4	+	2	+	1
+	2	+	6	+	7	+
4	+	3	+	5	+	4

152. Answers will vary but may be similar to:

	Player #1										Player #2							
1	2	③	4	5	6	⑦	⑧	⑨	**27**	9	⑧	⑦	6	5	④	3	②	1
1	2	3	4	5	⑥	7	8	⑨	**15**	9	⑧	⑦	6	5	4	3	2	1
①	2	3	4	5	6	7	⑧	⑨	**18**	9	8	⑦	⑥	⑤	4	3	2	1
1	②	3	4	5	⑥	⑦	⑧	⑨	**32**	⑨	⑧	⑦	6	⑤	4	3	②	①
①	2	3	④	⑤	⑥	⑦	⑧	⑨	**40**	⑨	⑧	⑦	⑥	5	④	③	②	①
①	2	3	4	5	⑥	⑦	⑧	⑨	**31**	⑨	⑧	⑦	⑥	⑤	④	3	2	①
1	2	3	4	5	6	7	⑧	⑨	**17**	9	8	⑦	6	5	④	③	②	①

Logic Puzzles

153. Alison's notebook only has spiral binding.

154. The horse does not belong because it does not start with a "p."

155.

Answer Key *(cont.)*

157. The frog does not belong because it does not start with an "m," nor does it have fur.

158.

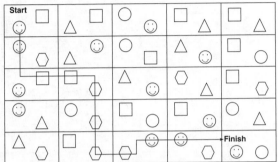

159.

160.

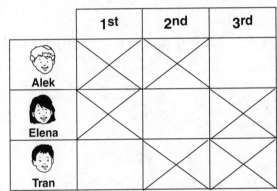

Which pet did Alek have? __the pig__

Which pet did Elena have? __the cat__

Which pet did Tran have? __the dog__

161. Lisa's sock only has polka dots on it.

162. The monkey does not belong because it is not a cat.

164. The lion does not belong because it is not a pet. Or, the rabbit does not belong because it hops.

165.

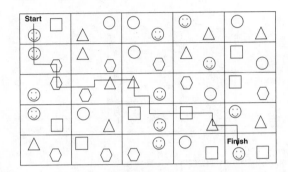

166.

	1st	2nd	3rd
Alek	✕	✕	
Elena	✕		✕
Tran		✕	✕

How did Alek finish the race? __in 3rd place__

How did Elena finish the race? __in 2nd place__

How did Tran finish the race? __in 1st place__

168.

What did Alek eat for lunch? __the salad__

What did Elena eat for lunch? __the sandwich__

What did Tran eat for lunch? __the hot dog__

Answer Key *(cont.)*

169. The eagle does not belong because it flies.

170.

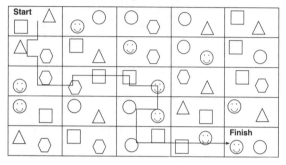

172.

173. Dan's kite only has stripes on it.

174. The penguin does not belong because it does not fly.

175.

177. Mike's snowman had a carrot nose, four buttons, and two branches for arms.

178. The spider does not belong because it has eight legs.

179.

180.

	Striped Shirt	Plain Shirt	Dotted Shirt
Alek			
Elena			
Tran			

What shirt did Alek wear? ___the dotted shirt___

What shirt did Elena wear? ___the plain shirt___

What shirt did Tran wear? ___the striped shirt___

181.

182. Tom's pizza has pepperoni and mushrooms on it.